WH

STUCK

BEING

WHO YOU'RE STUCK BEING

AN INTROSPECTIVE YEAR OF
HAIKU JOURNALING

MIKE DIGRAZIA

For Pepper
For my family
For my pals

INTRODUCTION

At the tail end of 2018, while dealing with some big life changes and trying my best to ride the wave of life's ups and downs, I decided that it would be a good idea to start journaling again.

IN CASE YOU DIDN'T KNOW...

A daily journal is a great tool for self-reflection. If done consistently, it has the potential to become a downright sacred space. A private space where you can explore your thoughts and feelings, ponder your hopes and dreams, examine your worries and fears and reflect on all the things in life you are most grateful for. If you've never tried it, give it a shot... all the *cool* kids are doing it!

To keep things interesting, I decided to document my thoughts in *haiku* form, instead of standard long-winded journal entries.

FOR THOSE UNFAMILIAR...

The *haiku* is a Japanese form of poetry consisting of three lines and 17 syllables. It's traditionally a 5-7-5 structure, meaning that the first line contains 5 syllables, the second line contains 7 syllables and the third line contains 5 syllables.

So that's what I did. For just over a year, I wrote AT LEAST one *haiku* journal entry every night. I enjoyed the process so much that, on occasional nights, I would write 10 or 15 at a time. I was vibing with the universe, man... and it probably had little or nothing to do with those evening cups of coffee that I arguably should not have been drinking at the time. No... seriously.

I finished that batch of *haiku* journaling right at the very beginning of 2020. The process had done what I had hoped it would do. It gave me something creative to occupy myself with while simultaneously helping me work through a considerable amount of internal *stuff*. Having fulfilled its purpose, I closed the journal and tucked it away. It would not be seen again until...

JANUARY, 2021

INT. MIKE'S GARAGE - DAY

MIKE grabs a small, battered moving box off the top of a large pile and plops it down on a nearby workbench. A Sharpie-scribbled message on the box reads, "SOME RANDOM SHIT AND PROBABLY SOME DICE".

He chuckles to himself, fumbles with the curled end of some packing tape and RIPS it off the box in one swift motion.

He peers into the box and begins digging out the pile of treasures inside... A THROWING STAR BELT BUCKLE tucked inside a TIBETAN SINGING BOWL... a stack of GODZILLA COMICS... a few SPIRITUAL BOOKS... three random DICE... and one YELLOW JOURNAL.

Yep. The yellow journal I pulled out of the box that day was the *haiku* journal itself, and a hell of a lot had changed since I had written my last entry at the start of 2020. In addition to finding myself now living on the opposite side of the country, Covid-19 had ravaged, and was continuing to ravage the world, causing unfathomable hardship and stress to the planet's population. In a heartbeat, everything had changed... for everyone.

When I pulled the journal out of that battered old moving box, I sat down and cracked it open for the first time in over a year. As I flipped through the pages and scanned through what I had written, I laughed to myself and smiled. Though the gist of everything I had written had no doubt been communicated before countless times throughout the ages, by folks far more eloquent than the likes of me, I found some genuine nuggets of optimistic positivity and truth in those words. And with everything going on in the world at that moment, reading it was just what I needed to get myself back on track.

So, that's why I decided to share the *haiku* journal with you. In the hope that it might inspire a sense of positivity or universality in a time rife with hardship and uncertainty.

I sincerely hope that you find it worth reading. If not, I promise it will look rad on your shelf.

Fist bumps and hugs,

- Mike DiGrazia

A NOTE ABOUT
THE FOLLOWING HAIKU

Traditionally, *haiku* are
displayed with spaces between lines.
In this collection, I have chosen to
discard the spaces between lines
for purely aesthetic reasons.

Additionally, all use and non-use
of punctuation and capitalization
is intentional.

**Are you being who
You really want to be, or
Who you're STUCK being?**

A river flowing
Consistently in motion
Be like a river

WHO YOU'RE STUCK BEING

**Sale in aisle 13
Preconceived notions abate
Everything must go**

Don't change what you see
Change the way that you see it
It's not all that bad

WHO YOU'RE STUCK BEING

**One cricket alone
Trills a new tune of its own
Still part of the choir**

Now I am ready
As ready as possible
To procrastinate

**A total shit show
Can be prime fertilizer
For the main event**

As we ride the wave
It becomes ever more clear
That we ARE the wave

WHO YOU'RE STUCK BEING

Let weary muscles
Relax into harmony
With the universe

See significance
In all you have accomplished
EVERYTHING matters

WHO YOU'RE STUCK BEING

**A body of cells
Functioning in unison
Against all the odds**

**Diaphanous thoughts
Doing their due diligence
Promoting healing**

WHO YOU'RE STUCK BEING

There's no I in TEAM
But there is a **TEAM** in **STEAM**
and a **FLU** in **FLUTE**

A complex array
of muscles, nerves and tendons
This strange soul vessel

WHO YOU'RE STUCK BEING

What good comes out of
You making the worst of a
Bad situation?

**Knowledge is power
Power is definitely
Rewop spelled backwards**

WHO YOU'RE STUCK BEING

Creativity
Conceptualization
Electricity

Sometimes you HAVE TO
Even if you don't WANT TO
Sometimes you HAVE TO

WHO YOU'RE STUCK BEING

**Do something today
To make someone feel at ease
and that they are loved**

Sometimes you need to
Claw and drag yourself out of
Your comfort bubble

WHO YOU'RE STUCK BEING

You're only human
But be the best possible
Human you can be

You know those **HANG-UPS?**
That's exactly what they are
They're only **HANG-UPS!**

A door you may close
May open a new one that
Smacks you in the face

Love can elevate
It can push you well beyond
Your perceived apex

WHO YOU'RE STUCK BEING

**All you really need
is that which you REALLY need
THAT is what you need**

Now that I know, I
Can say with all honesty
That I do not know

WHO YOU'RE STUCK BEING

**Synapses firing
You rise to the occasion
Your hands get to work**

In all honesty
I can honestly say that
I'm being honest

WHO YOU'RE STUCK BEING

**A person of strength
of wisdom and fortitude
What I shall become**

Coffee... NEMESIS!
Do your best. I can take it.
The battle is lost.

WHO YOU'RE STUCK BEING

You need to believe
You are fully capable
of rising above

The sun set today
With any luck it will set
Again tomorrow

WHO YOU'RE STUCK BEING

And so, just like that
Everything you know changes
And you change with it

A great confidence
and positive outlook blooms
like a minstrel's prose

**Recharging a must
Get horizontal post haste
Levels depleted**

Time to walk the walk
The walk of the talk of walk
Walk that walk of talk!

WHO YOU'RE STUCK BEING

Unconventional
How I feel in this moment
Defy conventions

All tied together
So many lives intertwined
Interdependent

WHO YOU'RE STUCK BEING

**Keep chipping away
Chip away all that you want
It's still part of you**

When your tide goes out
What gems will you
leave behind
For the world to find

**Be the brightest light
Shine as brightly as you can
Be a light... always**

I sit pondering
If I should be pandering
While meandering

WHO YOU'RE STUCK BEING

Look in the mirror
Who you see is not the you
You were yesterday

Don't wallow in them
Those emotional doldrums
Greet them and proceed

**Emotional trap
Oh, I see what you did there
I'm onto your game**

Here I consider
The politics of being
Quite considerate

WHO YOU'RE STUCK BEING

**This hokey bullshit...
Turns out it isn't at all
Not a single bit**

If you love yourself
It's easier to love more
and love more deeply

As bright as it gets
Brightness ceases to exist
If the darkness dies

Going with the flow
Riding the cosmic rhythm
And enjoying it

When that lightning strikes
Don't catch it in a bottle
Become the lightning

When it rains it pours
Turning stable ground to mud
Let your lotus grow

WHO YOU'RE STUCK BEING

The best kind of gift
That one can give to one's self
is the gift of peace

You may be right, or
Paradoxically wrong
It is what it is

Practice what I say
If you practice what I do
You'll say the same thing

What you're looking for
may or may not really be
the thing that you need

This whole ball of wax
What an awe-inspiring sight
When you look at it

**That anxiety
No matter how much you have
Won't change the outcome**

This silly construct
Made of meat, bone,
cells, tissue...
Piloted by what?

**Move past that time spent
Sinking deep into the past
It leaves you PAST TENSE!**

Sitting inside steel
Atop steel wheels
on steel beams
With a steely gaze

**Adventure awaits
So grab it by its tendrils
and ride, my friend... ride**

WHO YOU'RE STUCK BEING

Quite clearly I see
That absolutely nothing
Is quite clearly clear

You laugh at yourself
Laugh at all life throws at you
You laugh and you learn

Tension builds and builds
Using fear as its mortar
Despair as its bricks

Burnish your design
Even when you're
not quite sure
What the future holds

If I continue
Stay the course down
paths of old
What lies ahead then?

Feeling emboldened
I put my best foot forward
Horizons expand

So here we have it
Now what do we do with it
Now that we have it?

So, the smallest things
are often the biggest things
Live in those moments

All of that tension
Let it all go, my good friend
It serves no purpose

Constrained by the rules
Swimming inside
of our pools
Just a bunch of fools

WHO YOU'RE STUCK BEING

Within this here ink
Lies a measured tranmission
Of my cognition

Nurture compassion
For yourself and for the world
It's the only way

Escape your cocoon
There's much to experience
Outside your bubble

**If mental constructs
Are taken out of context
Who wins the contest?**

Love is where it's at
It is what it's all about
So keep on loving

**Inspiring others
To also inspire others
To inspire others**

WHO YOU'RE STUCK BEING

**You CAN Time Travel
Just follow your memories
And it's FREE to boot!**

**Superfluously
I ask another question
I know the answer**

WHO YOU'RE STUCK BEING

Not my best effort
If I do say so myself
Keep on winning, champ

I'm so befuddled
I can't honestly tell if
It's migraine or yours

WHO YOU'RE STUCK BEING

You really can be
That person you want to be
Before you can't be

**Do something right now!
What can you do this moment
To find happiness?**

**What are you doing
With the precious
time you have?
Anything at all?**

Digital savior
Tethered abomination
Consumer of time

In the darkest night
If I breathe and look deeply
I can see the light

I see the future
Shining bright in front of me
But can't see the now

WHO YOU'RE STUCK BEING

**The need to create
Profound desire to share it
It's imperative**

What can it all mean?
Is it all a can of beans?
This is what it seems

WHO YOU'RE STUCK BEING

Smile because you know
That deep down
you've always known
You already know

I know what to do
It's just so hard to do it
When you don't want to

You only live once
Be what you want to be, the
Best you can be it

Bask in the glory
Of all you have accomplished
Then get back to work

Trudge through the brain bog
Muse machete clears a path...
Path of creation

If we could all be
a cavalcade of buddhas
mindfully being...

You write your own book
Author your own adventure
Design your own arc

You're responsible
For your words
and your actions
You and you alone

WHO YOU'RE STUCK BEING

Remember your goals
Stamp them into your noodle
And manifest them

Say yes to more things
Say no to far far less things
And say less things more

**The end of one thing
The beginning of one thing
One thing... Always one**

When you're frustrated
Put your right head in and you
Shake it all about

WHO YOU'RE STUCK BEING

**Life is like a wave
It crests and falls just the same
Be the wave... BE it!**

Why don't you wake up
And smell what you shovelin'
Before you Die Hard

WHO YOU'RE STUCK BEING

Once in a great while
I stop and smell the roses
and they smell me back

I feel like a King
I mean like something heavy
Weighing on my head

The gloaming brings forth
The promise of a new night
and another day

**Be the best you can
Always be the best you can
Be the best Toucan**

Your ducks in a row
Get your damn ducks in a row
They are YOUR damn ducks

**Cultivate some love
Cultivate some compassion
Cultivate kindness**

WHO YOU'RE STUCK BEING

**Constantly yearning
For a little something more
The question is... what?**

Flash in the darkness
Momentarily mapping
A concealed pathway

WHO YOU'RE STUCK BEING

When you know you have
To put things in perspective
There's no need to not

**Stroking the ego
I fear that I've let ME go
Should we let WE go?**

WHO YOU'RE STUCK BEING

Tap into the joy
It's there deep down
inside you
Waiting to be found

This is your story
and these moments are canon
if you say they are

Completely spastic
Just a hopeless romantic
Who's feeling frantic

In a sea of change
Discovering my purpose
Also my porpoise

WHO YOU'RE STUCK BEING

So precious little
The amount of time we have
Make the most of it

Those IFS, ANDS and BUTS
And those WHYS
and WHENS and WHERES
Know not of the NOW

WHO YOU'RE STUCK BEING

**You dream of that day
and do whatever it takes
to make it happen**

**Be a warrior
Ready to conquer it all
When you feel you can't**

Every so often
You need to open your eyes
and see... see yourself

How can someone so
Uninspired be so inspired
It's so inspiring

WHO YOU'RE STUCK BEING

When things aren't the best
But they aren't
the worst either
It's not all that bad

**Do that thing you do
Where you go about doing
What needs to be done**

**So nice to see you,
My dear old pal exhaustion
It's been way too soon**

Sitting on the brink
Of a glowing new frontier
Facing it with poise

What it comes down to
is that we are all the same
The whole lot of us

Facing the unknown
Embracing it with a smile
Old fears melt away

You know what pain is?
The opposite of non-pain
One needs the other

Transitional space
Lingering for far too long
As life passes by

WHO YOU'RE STUCK BEING

Be the change you want
To see in the world today
Become that change NOW

Can't make an omelette
Without the intention to
Make a damn omelette

Can I maintain it,
This sense of wonder
and light?
Is it possible?

On the horizon
A radiant sun rises
This very moment

I look back at him
The person I used to be
I hug him and laugh

Year of clear vision
Not too far in the distance
The future is bright

WHO YOU'RE STUCK BEING

Maple maple mape
Maple maple maple mape
Mapetty mape mape

Clothes made of earth stuff
Earth stuff made
of cosmos stuff
It's ALL the same stuff

WHO YOU'RE STUCK BEING

**Stop judging yourself
Accepting that you are flawed
Is half the battle**

**The truth will come out
Once you are ready to be
Truthful with yourself**

And a flame goes out
Gone, but still there in a sense
Eternally there

Too tired to think straight
Maybe I should think sideways
Or outside the box

**Beauty. Everywhere.
Just look and you will find it,
waiting to be seen.**

A fallen leaf sits
Alone, but for a moment
Wind summons good friends

**Collective of light
Pulsing though the universe
Radiating love**

**Yes, caterpillar
Not only do I see you
I know your future**

WHO YOU'RE STUCK BEING

**Dubiously I
Continue to chart my course
Into the unknown**

You flow with the wave
Ups and downs
and ins and outs
You find peace within

WHO YOU'RE STUCK BEING

Elixir of life
Culled from the
ground below us
Abundance of gifts

Thank you to the rain
Whose soothing intelligence
Calms the weary soul

Smile. Just smile and breathe.
Breathe and smile,
and breathe again.
Take the time you need.

Please check your baggage
And carry on your journey
Lighter and carefree

WHO YOU'RE STUCK BEING

Tires roll through darkness
High beams cut straight
through the void
Ever winding roads

I hear the ocean
After flushing the toilet
Hisses to silence

This bundle of nerves
Has driven this soul enough
It's my turn to drive

**Make your dream come true
No matter what it might take
To realize it**

**Emerson was right
But I'm not so sure about
That Lake and Palmer**

When all's said and done
Let me posit this question
What is it YOU'VE done?

Sure, we all must rest
But remember that one day
We sleep eternal

Your will of iron
Can't and will never be bent
Strength is in your veins

Stomach tied in knotts
What does the future entail?
The future will be

Mammoth clouds above
Glide effortlessly forward
Serene majesty

Magic button wand
Bring forth that which I desire
to fill bloodshot eyes

**Get back on the track
It's straight, it's narrow,
it's clear
Just get back on it!**

WHO YOU'RE STUCK BEING

Terror in the isles
The isles of
free-flowing thoughts
Left unchecked again

Those grudges you keep
They're likely
keeping you warm
While burning you up

**What a bunch of crap!
Positive affirmations...
Crap helps flowers grow**

Hello, good fortune
Glad to meet
your acquaintance
Sit down, stay a while

That place where you run
To be done with the running
Is running your life

When worries arise
Recognize them,
greet them and
Let them float on by

**Step out of the box
Every once in a great while
And see what's beyond**

At the root of it
Your seeds have
been neglegted
So just water them

Eat it, Comfort Zone!
I am kissing you goodbye
Onward and upward

**Time to get cosmic
Time to feel the vibration
Get into the flow**

WHO YOU'RE STUCK BEING

**Come home to yourself.
Be calm. Be still. Be tranquil.
Just relax and BE.**

**Stop focusing on
Your cultivated bullshit
And grow some insight**

**Carry on, my friend!
Just don't carry on about
That useless baggage**

When you're feeling lost
and you don't know
where to turn
Take one step forward

Like a bouncing ball
Ups, downs, ups, downs,
ups, downs, ups
Let's end with the ups

You're the one in charge
Of deciding who you are
And who you will be

WHO YOU'RE STUCK BEING

It's all amazing
Every conceivable bit
YOU are amazing!

Ah, yes... Here I am!
Where have I been all my life?
It's great to see me!

WHO YOU'RE STUCK BEING

Now is where it's at
If you're still looking for it
Where it's at is now

**Do something you love
Somehow, some time
and somewhere
Do something you love**

Here I am facing
A future I failed to see
With eyes open wide

The universe smiles
Then it throws daggers
Then it smiles again

WHO YOU'RE STUCK BEING

**You have the power
To control the way in which
You perceive yourself**

See who you once **WERE**
See who you **ARE** this moment
See who you **CAN BE**

Time for creation
Breathe life into
something good
Something wonderful

**You may not always
Have it there in your pocket
But change is constant**

Question all of it
Question why you question it
Then you question that

We are our parents
And their parents before them
For infinity

**Roar of an engine
Redlining in the distance
As I sit idling**

It's great to have friends
To lift you up when
you're down
And to watch flicks with

**So much emotion
Ignoring it and hiding
Behind nostalgia**

**Cultivate oneness
We are part of the same thing
All of us are IT**

**Stress is reaction
Choose not to react poorly
Diminish the stress**

Rise from the ashes
like a Phoenix of legend
You can be reborn

Spiraling tunnel
Lights, colors, interwoven
Saturated dreams

**The real champion
Is the one who can control
What they are thinking**

Some days you got it
Some days you
wish you had it
But all days are days

You can be two things
Positive or negative
Which one will you choose?

If you have an "I"
And I have an "I"
Are we both the "I"?

Don't just **THINK** you can
KNOW you can
with all your heart
KNOW IT and **DO IT**

**Fortified mountain
Stable as the day is long
Unbreakable will**

It's so elusive
That thing that you're
looking for
But IT will find YOU

WHO YOU'RE STUCK BEING

**To acknowledge who
You are is so refreshing
Like acknowledgeMINTS**

Spend less time talking
Try spending that time doing
And see what happens

WHO YOU'RE STUCK BEING

Imagination
Can unlock your potential
Great things await you

I am forever
Grateful for what I have had
And all that I will

**Sit... Quiet your mind...
Looking deeply you can see
The way things CAN be**

Life is like jello
It wiggles and it wobbles
And it's delicious

**Spout brings water forth
The water was there waiting
Long before the spout**

**You're the one in charge
Of your body and your brain
Tell it what to do**

A wonderful thing
This cosmic community
That we are part of

Apocalyptic
Sometimes that's
the way it seems
But you know the truth

WHO YOU'RE STUCK BEING

**When life gets you down
Look up and remember this...
You're alive... ALIVE!**

**Inner dialogue
You really need to shut it
Your pie hole, that is**

WHO YOU'RE STUCK BEING

Feel the happiness
It's right there,
deep down inside
Ready to be found

Though it takes one cog
To throw a clock off balance
It can be replaced

WHO YOU'RE STUCK BEING

Be ridiculous
As often as possible
Youth lives in your heart

You can stagnate in
The land of good intentions
Or make it happen

**Transformational
That's one way to describe it
Embracing insight**

So much cinnamon
So so so much cinnamon
Too much cinnamon

**All of this turmoil
Yet the clouds still float on by
And the sun still shines**

What are the chances
Drinking that big soda was
A good idea?

WHO YOU'RE STUCK BEING

**Laugh! Laugh at it all!
Because it is what it is
And that's all it is**

Sink into it now
Sink into that warm embrace
Glorious coffee

WHO YOU'RE STUCK BEING

**This grand game of life
Is just waiting to be played
So PLAY, my friend. PLAY!**

A smile. Just one smile.
Is all that it takes to melt
A frozen blood pump.

**Be a ray of hope
Be a shining example
Of love and kindness**

**Make a difference
If it's the last thing you do
Make a difference**

**Positivity
Has gone straight
out the window
To be continued...**

Coming back online...
My OS reformatted
Upgraded system

My brain is scrambled
With the right ingredients
A seasoned omelette

**Does that shit matter?
Can focusing on it change
Anything at all?**

WHO YOU'RE STUCK BEING

When your pen dies out
Give it a couple of shakes
Bring it back to life

**Is it possible
To do the impossible?
Well, yes. Possibly.**

BOOK RECOMMENDATIONS

There are many books that have inspired me over the years. Some of which undoubtedly, in some way or another, inspired the headspace I was in while writing the *haiku* in this book. The following are a few especially good ones:

AT HOME IN THE WORLD *by Thich Nhat Hanh*

NO DEATH, NO FEAR *by Thich Nhat Hanh*

FEAR *by Thich Nhat Hanh*

POLISHING THE MIRROR *by Ram Dass*

THE DAILY STOIC *by Ryan Holiday*

MEDITATIONS *by Marcus Aurelius*

THE MISSION OF ART *by Alex Grey*

INFINITE POTENTIAL *by Mitch Horowitz*

THE MIRACLE HABITS *by Mitch Horowitz*

THE FOUR AGREEMENTS *by Don Miguel Ruiz*

THE MEDICINE BAG *by Don Jose Ruiz*

WISDOM OF THE SHAMANS *by Don Jose Ruiz*

**THE ADVENTURES OF BUCKAROO BANZAI
ACROSS THE EIGHTH DIMENSION** *by Earl Mac Rauch*

**A CRITICAL HISTORY AND FILMOGRAPHY
OF TOHO'S GODZILLA SERIES** *by David Kalat*

ABOUT MIKE DIGRAZIA

MIKE DIGRAZIA is a creator of stuff and a maker of things who has an affinity for gobbledygook. He lives in Phoenix, and on good days, aspires to be one.

SEE MIKE'S ART

www.digraziart.com

LISTEN TO MIKE'S MUSIC

pozitivytron.bandcamp.com

FOLLOW MIKE

 **digraziart**

WATCH FOR THE
NEXT ADVENTURE
OF
MIKE DIGRAZIA

SOME RANDOM SHIT
AND PROBABLY SOME DICE

Made in the USA
Las Vegas, NV
17 January 2024

84250375R00152